Bertie's Diary

To Jaz

Enjoy!

Best Wishes,

Davina Baron

Davina Baron

xxx

Published by East Anglian Press

British Library Cataloguing in Publication Data.
A CIP catalogue record for this book is available from the British Library.

ISBN: 978-0-9954844-9-8

Acknowledgements

Special thanks to

Enrico Baroni for his relentless encouragement

Julie Durrant for her support and grammar skills

Suzan Collins for 'hounding' me and making this possible

the inspirational Sue Townsend

– and, finally, to Bertie Boy who was my dearest companion for eleven years. Still miss you Berts!

Illustrator: Vivienne Baroni

Contents   Page

Introducing Me

I didn't get to know my real mum that well. I had six brothers and sisters and I was always the last to find a place to feed from her, by which time she'd had enough of us pulling her about, and usually tried to walk away with me still hanging on for dear life! As soon as we all started eating from a bowl, she disappeared from our lives and I never saw her again.

We shared a run with some spaniel puppies, which was not much fun as they were all a bit thick and fat. Neither my brothers and sisters nor the spaniel puppies took much notice of me as I was very small and easily squashed. In fact, the puppy run was a miserable place to be and I would have cried all day long if it weren't for my dad.

My dad is a handsome dachshund, long haired and well-groomed with a fantastic tail. He told me that he'd won a petition and had a cup with his name on it, (I'd have rather had a bowl as cups tip over when you try to drink out of them), which was why me and my brothers and sisters were special. Although, I am more special because I am the smallest.

Dad came to the run each day to see how I was getting on and to tell me clever things to remember for when a human came to collect me. And that day was not too far off apparently!

Human Day

paper payment thing

Spotty
(looking pleased)

I've been stuck in this run with some yapping spaniel puppy all week and I'm sick of her. I keep telling her that I haven't been stretched – I'm a dachshund and a miniature one, at that. My perfect physique, combined with my beautiful red coat, means that I will remain a loveable little dog, while she will get bigger and get on everyone's nerves and in their way.

I'm now ten weeks old and should be getting a human of my own very soon. All my siblings have been taken away by some very strange looking humans and I just hope, when the time comes, mine's presentable. My dad said that there's nothing worse than having to walk down the road with an ugly human; it's embarrassing. He's very clever, my dad, and visits our run every day to tell me important things because I'm special.

Just as stupid spaniel puppy is, once again, trying to get her nose stuck up my bum, and I'm contemplating biting one of her flappy ears, a woman approaches our run with Spotty, the fat kennel maid. I immediately adopt my adorable 'get me out of here' pose and Spotty picks me up and hands me to the woman. She loves me straightaway, I can tell, and she smells nice so I nibble her ear. She's presentable, too. Nice hair and big, brown eyes, bit like mine really, and she's wearing a long, flowery skirt. Dad would approve.

'Oh, he's gorgeous,' says the woman, and so I wag my tail even harder and lick her neck. She's holding me like she's never going to put me down and I feel an instant bonding. Then all three of us set off for the office while stupid spaniel puppy yaps her head off and tries to climb the run fence.

'Tat ta, stupid spaniel puppy. You'll look far more appealing, now, without me stuck on the end of your nose.' She looked puzzled but that's only to be expected; spaniels are such late developers.

In the office, nice woman struggles to write out a small piece of paper with numbers on it - I'm still in her arms, you see – and gives it to Spotty. My dad says that piece of paper means the human will love and cherish you forever, even when you wee on the carpet. Then Spotty gets a big box with holes in it and nice woman puts me inside. Then, for heaven's sake, they closed the top and everything went dark. I yelped like mad.

'He'll be fine in there until you get home. You don't have far to go, do you?' Think again, Spotty. I'm not fine and I might just do a poo to prove it.

'Only a couple of miles and my car's just around the corner.' What's a car?

A car is a moving thing that humans sit in and it takes them places, I later find out. Nice woman is chatting away to me as the car thing is moving and I decide not to do the poo. She tells me her name is Hannah and she is my new mum and that we're going home. I'm still yapping away inside the box and feel a bit sick. I think it's the moving car. No point not doing the poo and then being sick. So, I push the top of the box as hard as I can with my head and, hoorah, my head pokes out and, bloody hell, things outside the car are whizzing past like no dog's business. Newmum laughs and pats my head.

'We're nearly there. Just stay still. Won't be long now.' I quite like the car thing now that I can see, and just make the occasional yap, sort of conversational like.

The car stops and Newmum gets out. Hey, what about me, I think, and then she comes around to my side and opens the car and lifts out the box.

'Here we are, Bertie. We're home.' One small thing, who the hell is Bertie?

Cat Day

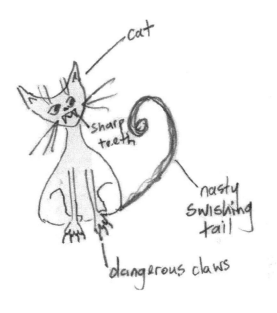

What a busy couple of days I've had. Got the 'Bertie' business sorted out. That's me, my new name and I quite like it, rather distinguished don't you think. Newmum has a mate, a big fella with huge feet. I'm going to have to watch that one, as the house doesn't seem to be big enough for him, his feet and me.

Just one big problem. The cat. And he's black, fat, lazy, and very big, and not in a cage. Where I was born, there were cats and they were always in cages. My dad said this was because they tell lies and scratch humans, and their humans had gone somewhere to have holidays and fun to feel better. For some reason that escapes me, Newmum thought the cat would like me and would fuss over me as though I was a funny shaped kitten. Think again, Newmum. He thought I looked more like a rat and said I stink, and I told him that was rich coming from something that smells like rotten fish. Then he whacked me across the nose and made it bleed. Result: Newmum whacked him and sent him to the shed while I whimpered, realistically I thought, in her arms.

Newmum works at home, upstairs, in front of a box thing with lights she calls a pewter, and she's put a comfortable cushion near her desk, in front of the fire, just for me. And when I get fed up with that, I jump up at her legs and she puts me on her lap, and then struggles to tip tap on the pewter because I'm licking her face.

Spotty had given Newmum a list of my dietary requirements, which she must have made up because I've never had any of this revolting stuff before. Scrambled egg is horrid and tinned rice pudding is for wimps. Newmum threw the list away this morning and we had a bacon sandwich.

The sleeping arrangements are not to my liking as I must spend the nights in a kennel cage in the kitchen. It's not the cage I object to, it's quite cosy and I have three blankets; no, it's the taunting and spitting from the cat that gets on my nerves. Niko, (bit of a fancy name for a big fat black cat born and bred in Dagenham, I thought), even sprayed in my face last night and it took me ages to wash off the smell. My dad had warned me about cats and their sprays. He said when you see them lift up their tails and squeeze their bums, run for it before you get a face full of the stinky stuff. But, in the cage, I can't 'run for it', so have come up with a plan for tonight and then it's no more night time, bullying moggy for me.

A Sun Day

Hoorah for me! My plan worked perfectly and I am now safely cuddled up in the duvet with Newmum, listening to the Archers Omnibus. I like Radio Four. My dad said Radio Four was for intelligent dogs, such as us and German

Shepherds, and that Radio One was for the likes of stupid spaniel puppy and Yorkies. Perhaps that's why they all yap so much.

Back to my plan. Newmum put me in my kennel cage last night, as usual, turned off the lights and went upstairs to bed. I waited for a few minutes and then I howled and howled. It was a pitiful sound – one of my best, I thought. I could hear Newmum coming down the stairs, so I quickly grabbed my water bowl and tipped the water just outside my cage and called out to Niko, 'Hey, Fish Face. Smell my bum!'

And, yes, you guessed it. The Big Fat Black Cat sprang from the living room and attacked my cage, just as Newmum turned on the kitchen light.

'Bad puss. Leave Bertie alone.' I smirked at the BFBC, whined, and pawed at the side of my cage to draw Newmum's attention to the puddle on the floor. 'Oh, you naughty, naughty boy. Did you do that? Fancy weeing up

Bertie's cage. Get out. Go on.' Such a satisfying sight; Niko's bum disappearing through the cat-flap out into the dark, cold night. And I think I can hear rain.

Newmum cleared up the 'wee' and then opened my cage and took me into her arms. 'Oh, you poor boy. Did that nasty puss frighten you? Come on, you're coming upstairs with me.'

We didn't make a sound as we crept into the bedroom and me and Newmum got comfy in bed. Big Fella was still awake.

'Is Bertie okay now? He's gone very quiet.' Then he turned over and I licked his face. 'Aargh! You can't let him sleep up here. He'll never settle downstairs if you do that.'

'It's just for tonight. Niko scared him and weed up his cage. Bertie's only a baby, after all.'

'On your head, be it.' And, before long, Big Fella is snoring very loudly. My dad said that some humans make this snorting, growly sound when they are sleeping and it means 'please poke me in the back', which I do and nothing happens. I don't understand this snoring business or its purpose. It is very annoying and I'll have to deal with it another time.

After a lovely night's sleep, I woke up to tea and toast. Big Fella had got up early, leaving me to sprawl across the warm place he'd left, and then he came back with the tea and toast for Newmum. I was not left out and, before long, I was lapping at some tea from her saucer, which nicely washed down my mouthfuls of toast. Suddenly, I remembered my puppy bladder and danced around on the bed, making cute little whining sounds, and Newmum told Big Fella to take me downstairs to the garden.

It was wet outside and I don't cock my leg yet, so I had to squat in the rain, while holding my tail up at the same time. You try it. It's not easy.

Suitably relieved, I was taken back upstairs to Newmum, the duvet, warm tea and toast, and The Archers. I like Sun days.

Later, Newmum was making food in this big hot cupboard called an oven. The smell was making me dribble. I have a cushion in the kitchen, right near the hot cupboard, where I can sit and watch Newmum as she does all sorts of things, including opening a tin of some smelly muck for the cat as he purrs and wraps his tail around her legs. I whimper and wag my tail, not because I want the smelly muck, I just want Newmum to remember that she loves me the best.

'You'll get yours soon, silly boy,' she says in that funny voice she has recently adopted for talking to me. 'It's chicken – you'll like that.' Too right, I will, but you'd better get a move on, my tummy's rumbling like mad.

Eventually, my dinner arrives and I stick my nose in the bowl. What's this?

My lovely chicken dinner has bits in it! Green and orange ones. Sorry, Newmum, I don't do green and orange bits. So, I carefully lift them all out and leave them in a little pile beside the bowl, and then scoff my chicken.

'Oh, look! Little Berts doesn't like his vegetables, do you boy?' No I don't and I wag my tail and beg to be picked up and cuddled. 'You'll get used to them, Bertie.' Oh no I won't! In my opinion, they belong in the same category as scrambled egg and tinned rice pudding.

Vet Day

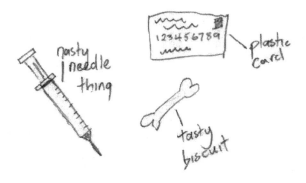

Had a wee bit of a shock today. This morning, Newmum got a pet carrier out of the cupboard and put it in the hall. (The beginning of the week had gone very well, I thought, and I'm gradually getting everyone to come around to my way of thinking, even me and Niko have come to an understanding: if I get too close to him, he whacks me across the nose when Newmum isn't looking).

When Niko saw the pet carrier, he sniggered in a hissy sort of way that made my hackles tingle.

'I knew you wouldn't be here for long, Scraggy Puppy. Do you know what the pet carrier means? Of course you don't, I can tell by your stupid little face. That's the trouble with eyebrows, they give away your every thought.' The Big Fat Black Cat then jumped onto the settee and curled up and started to purr.

'What do you mean, Fish Face? I'm not going anywhere. I'm not! What do you mean? Tell me, tell me,' and I jumped up at the settee and breathed on his face, wagging my tale furiously. A bit of a stupid thing to do really, but I was confused.

'He who gets put into the pet carrier is never seen again, Scraggy Puppy. I know this because it happened to my mother. One day she was here and the next, into the pet carrier and gone. I didn't mind too much because she was old and moaned a lot and used to eat all the crunchy dry food before I had the chance to taste it. Now, unless you want another whack across the nose, get your smelly face away from mine and let me sleep.'

I whined. What had I done? This wasn't the way my dad said things would turn out. And then Newmum came into the room and picked me up and put me into the pet carrier. I cried like hell.

'Don't be silly, Bertie,' she said. 'You won't be in there long. We're only going to the vet's.'

The vet's. Well, that was all right then. I stopped crying and sighed heavily. I knew what the vet was, he used to come to the kennels, a nice chap who feels your chest, looks at your willy and then gives you a biscuit.

As Newmum picked up the carrier and headed for the front door, I yelled out to the BFBC, 'See you later, Fish Face. Keep the settee warm for me.' He then said something very rude.

At the vet's, Newmum took me out of the carrier and held me in her arms. I have this endearing way of hanging my head over her shoulder when being held and so, head positioned and big brown eyes fixed with a look of suitable apprehension, I surveyed the waiting room. Of course, everyone in the waiting room said I was beautiful and all went 'Aah' when I licked Newmum's face. Everyone, that is, except the miserable old mongrel sitting in the corner who just ignored me. Perhaps he is going blind or has catajacks. My dad said that some dogs get catajacks in their eyes when they get old.

Eventually, the vet called us into his poking room and Newmum put me on the table and told me to be a good boy. Of course I was going to be a good boy. I was going to have my willy looked at and get a biscuit. Well, I was right about the willy but wasn't expecting the rest. The vet looked in my ears and felt my legs, back and tail, and then he put me on some rubber platform and told Newmum that I was sick pound, and that I could have half the worming tablet. Sick pound sounds like a nasty disease but it isn't; it's a way of saying how big I am. And then, yeowser! The vet stuck a sharp thing in the skin of my neck and I cried out loud. Newmum picked me up and cuddled me and then thanked the stupid man for hurting me and apologised for the wee I had just done on the table.

'Oh, don't worry about that. The little chap was very brave, weren't you, boy?' Yes, I bloody well was. 'Do you have any problems with the puppy at the moment?'

'Not really. Well, just one thing. He won't eat any vegetables or puppy food, just chicken. So, I was wondering if I should be using a supplement?'

'These little dogs are notoriously fussy eaters and bossy to boot,' he said. Bloody cheek! 'Remember, you're in charge, not him. Try to break him of this sort of eating behaviour while he's still a puppy.' The vet is now beginning to get on my nerves, as I am very happy with my eating habits and do not feel that we need to 'break' them. 'Look, try him on these, it's a complete dry puppy food,' and he offered me some yucky, little, brown crunchy bits. I ate the crunchy bits just so that we could get out of there as I'd had enough of this vet and his unfounded opinions.

Back in the waiting room, Newmum was looking at the toy stand. This was promising, as I don't have any real toys at the moment, just a flannel and a pair of socks I pinched from the bathroom. She picked up this big black and white thing called a 'Harry Humbug' and pressed it. Hoorah. It made a lovely squeaky noise and I wagged my tail.

'We'll have this one,' said Newmum, 'because he's been such a good boy.' And she handed it to the girl behind the desk.

'It's bigger than him,' laughed the girl as she gave Newmum a piece of paper. I don't know what was on the piece of paper but it made Newmum's eyes go very big.

'I'll have to put all this on my credit card,' said Newmum and she gave the girl a piece of plastic.

'I know it seems like a lot, but it's better to be safe than sorry when it comes to their injections.' I had a nasty feeling that Newmum was compensating these people in some way for hurting me in the neck, but I had Harry Humbug so I didn't make a fuss.

Back home, I ran up the hall, dragging Harry Humbug with me, and bumped straight into the BFBC who screeched at the sight of Harry, and shot into the kitchen and out through the cat flap. Another good day, I think.

ME
(laughing)

catflap   EEEK!!

BFBC
Bum

SQUEAK!!

SQUEAK!!

my "Harry Humbug"

31

Lipstick and Hoover Day

YEOWZER!

Newmum has gone upstairs again to work on her pewter leaving me down here with only the Big Fat Black Cat to talk to, and he's managed to get the best chair. Just as well really as I'm still a bit damp and, even if I say so myself, a bit whiffy! Still, I like it.

Newmum is so fussy about things like that, always spraying the settee with some smelly stuff, and what's with this

'Put your lipstick away' business for dog's sake? I have a good romp around the garden in the rain, then she grabs me when I come in and rubs me all over with that old tea towel, I'm feeling good and so it's bound to pop out, isn't it? Just popped out again actually, just thinking about it, but she's not here to see it so, a quick lick and, oooh, that's lovely.

The BFBC is staring at me now through half open eyes and he's only jealous because Newmum had him 'done', whatever that means, a few years ago, and he says he's never been the same since. Must've been something awful because he wees on the carpet every time Newmum gets the pet carrier out of the cupboard!

Now me, I have this thing about the Hoover. Happened when I was just a pup. Newmum got it out, plugged it in and started whooshing it up and down the hall. Well, the wire was flapping and wiggling about all over the place so I jumped it, wrestled with it, and then bit it real hard like. Yeowser! Burning pain through my gums and my tail shot up like a flagpole. Then I legged it! Just ran and ran to the end of the garden, making as much noise as I could, and Newmum ran after me and grabbed me and cuddled me and rubbed me and, that's right, the 'lipstick' popped out but she didn't seem to mind that time. It was all okay though, I got pampered all day, had warm milk and honey, 'for the shock' Newmum said, and even the BFBC had to get out of the way so I could have my cushion right slap bang in front of the fire.

These days, whenever I see the Hoover thing, vroom! I'm off, heading for the bottom of the garden, end of the hall, anywhere just so that it can't see me and I can't see it. Not that it comes out very often because the Big Fella has been given that job and he can't see properly so he doesn't notice the mess. No, it doesn't come out much at all, unlike my 'lipstick' which pops out all the time. Ooops! There it goes again!

Engle Day

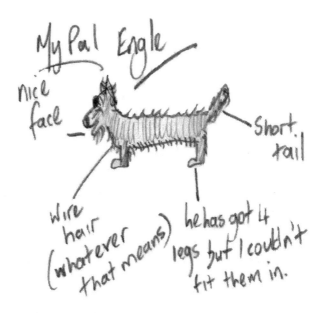

My Pal Engle

nice face

Short tail

Wire hair (whatever that means)

he has got 4 legs but I couldn't fit them in.

Newmum and Big Fella were very busy this morning, cleaning everywhere while me and Big Fat Black Cat Niko were shut out in the garden. I stayed near the back door, just in case he whacked me, then I could howl out in pain and Newmum would hear me.

I got a little bored, just hanging about, so went over to a large trough thing sitting against the garden wall to investigate its contents. I reached up to look inside and found it was filled with dirt. How marvellous! So, I jumped up into it for a little romp. Oh dear. It wasn't just filled with dirt. In fact, most of it was muddy water, but worth a romp just the same. I splashed in it and rolled in it and was having a thoroughly splendid time when the back door opened and Newmum came out to find me.

'Bertie! What are you doing? Oh no! Come and see what he's done,' she called out to the Big Fella. 'You silly boy. You're filthy. Oh, just what am I going to do with you? You're covered in mud. No, no, shut the door! Quickly! He can't go in like this. We've just cleaned up everywhere. Bertie, stay there!' Newmum was not pleased, I could tell, and she walked around the corner of the house and came back with a long green tube thing. 'You hold him and I'll spray him.' Spray! Humans don't spray! Only cats spray!

With that, Big Fella held me by my collar and Newmum aimed the green tube at me and squirted me all over with ice-cold water!

When the dousing was over, I immediately rolled onto my back and pawed the air frantically. My dad said this shows that you submit, even when it's not your fault, although it's a bit unnerving, exposing all your special bits. Newmum then fetched a towel and rubbed me all over and, yes, 'it' popped out.

'And you can put your lipstick away, you naughty boy,' she said, as she carried on rubbing me dry. I wasn't altogether in control of 'it' and so she flicked my willy and hissed 'Put it away!' I made a mental note of this for future reference: Newmum can be quite mean when it comes to my 'Lipstick'.

Once dry, I was allowed back into the kitchen, which was very clean and smelt funny, so I ran about sniffing at the cupboards and floor. It was the same in the living room, even my cushion had a strange whiff about it. In fact, the whole house seemed different, dirt-free and smelling rather sickly in my opinion.

Then the doorbell rang and I rushed to the front door, barking as loud as I could. My dad said that when you're a small dog you must bark as loudly as possible when the doorbell rings, so that the person on the other side of the door thinks you are very big and is scared. But I wasn't expecting to hear just as loud barking coming from the other side and was glad when Newmum picked me up before she opened the door.

And that's when I came face to face, for the first time, with Engle, a very scruffy looking little dachshund, who was soon to become my most bestest friend in the whole wide world.

'Hi Mum. Hi Dad. So lovely to see you. How was the journey? Yes, yes, Engle, you're a lovely boy. Look Bertie, this is Engle.' Then, Newmum put me down and that was it. Me and Engle sniffed each other's bottoms, and then galloped down the hall through to the living room, barking and jumping at each other. On reaching the kitchen, Big Fella opened the back door and we pelted out into the garden. Engle immediately spied the Big Fat Black Cat and chased him through the bushes.

'Can't stand cats,' panted Engle. 'Only thing they're good for is a bit of exercise. How you doing? Settling in okay? You're a handsome pup. I've never seen a long-haired before.'

'Thanks. Yeah, things here are fine and my new mum's lovely. So, what kind are you?' I had a great feeling about this brave, scampy looking dachshund.

'I'm a wire-haired. Great for swimming. Hey, come on. Race you round the shed.' I had no idea what 'swimming' was and before I could ask we were off again, running around the shed and making the occasional prancing leap at Niko, who was still hiding in the bushes. Now it was his turn to be scared.

Beach Day

Now, this all gets very confusing. Engle's human mum and dad are Newmum's mum and dad and Newmum's mum and dad told Engle that Newmum is his auntie, whatever that is, and I am his cushion. I think they may be old and have the beginnings of catajacks.

Engle and his humans are staying with us because it's sunny and we live near the beach. My dad said that the beach is a great place to run and play because it's soft and warm, and there's always lots to eat. I have never been to the beach and am very excited because we are all going there today. Newmum has put lots of chicken and other things into a large basket to take with us. (For a nasty minute there, I thought the basket meant another trip to the vet's). The BFBC isn't coming because, according to Engle, going to the beach is a holiday fun thing to do and cats are not allowed.

We all got into the car after Newmum had put the basket of chicken into the car thing's boot, which looks nothing like a boot and you can't chew it. Me and Engle sat in the back on our mums' laps so that we could look out of the windows. The car started to move and we were all very happy to be doing a holiday fun thing without Niko.

After a while, the car stopped and we all got out. Big Fella took the basket of chicken from the car boot and we walked up a small hill in the direction of some loud, swashing sound and, on reaching the top, I yelped in surprise at what I saw. In front of me was a lot of yellow stuff and beyond that was the biggest puddle I had ever seen - so big that you couldn't see the other side of it.

Newmum pulled at my lead to get me to step on the yellow stuff. Oh, it was lovely! So soft and warm on my paws. My dad was right and, of course, we had our chicken.

Me and Engle rolled in the yellow stuff, which Engle said was called sand, and then trotted along with the others to find a nice place to sit and eat the chicken. Newmum put down a blanket and sat on it while Big Fella placed the chicken basket beside her - and started to take his clothes off! So did Engle's mum and dad! They must have been very hot!

'Come on, Bertie,' said Big Fella. 'Race you to the sea!' And with that he started running towards the big puddle, followed by Engle and Engle's mum and dad.

'How about a paddle, then, Berts?' said Newmum, as she stood up and started walking after the others, dragging me along behind. 'It's a bit cold at first but you'll soon get used to it.'

Well, I've seen some strange things but nothing to compare with this. Engle was moving around in the puddle with his head just above the surface, so it must have been quite deep, furiously flapping his front paws, while the humans were splashing about in a ridiculous manner.

'Come on in for a swim, Bertie!' yelled Engle. 'The water's lovely!'

'I'm okay here, actually,' I called to him, just as the puddle surged over my paws and I jumped backwards in surprise. Swimming, I realised, meant getting very wet and cold, and definitely not for me.

'Oh, Berts! You're just like me. Not into swimming, eh? Bit too cold and wet.' And, to my relief, me and Newmum started back across the sand towards the blanket and the chicken. I'd been to the puddle, walked on the nice soft, warm sand and now I wanted to eat.

Sometime later, the swimmers came back to our blanket and shook water and sand all over everything, including me, and then Newmum opened the chicken basket. I was a little disappointed to discover that the basket was not full of chicken by any means, and that there was a distinct whiff of green and orange bits coming from somewhere. I needn't have worried, however, as me and Engle were soon tucking into plates of chicken and lapping at bowls of ice cold water, while the humans forced themselves to eat green and orange bits. Perhaps they are not allowed to have fun all day.

The sand had got very hot so I decided to have a little dig and discovered, under the hot stuff, was some cool, damp sand. Marvellous! I had just dug myself a nice little hole, (sending sand up over everyone which made them laugh for some reason), and was about to snuggle down when Engle plopped himself into it.

'Cheers, Berts. Just the spot for an afternoon snooze,' he said and, again, the humans all laughed.

'Look! Engle's pinched Bertie's cool spot,' said Newmum. 'Poor Bertie. You'll have to dig another one, sweetie.' So I did and, would you believe, Engle took over that one as well! Everyone positively honked with laughter and I was thinking that I'd had enough of this holiday fun thing!

'Hey! Come on, mate! Don't get all puppity,' said Engle. 'Dig another one and I promise I won't pinch it.'

'Alright then. And you'd better not 'cos I'm getting a bit upset and might have to growl at you.' My next hole was much better than the other two.

When we arrived home later that afternoon, I rushed up the hall to find Niko to tell him about the wonderful holiday fun thing we had done without him. He was pretending to be asleep on the settee so I told him anyway, but I left out the bit about the holes.

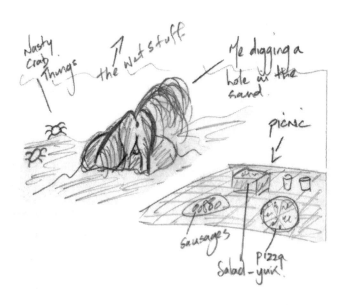

Naughty Car Day

lovely drippy whippy cornets!

hot sun

It was a sweltering summer's day and I was getting all hot and sweaty around the nether regions in this daytime heat when Nanny knocked at the door. She asked Newmum if she could take me out in their car to the beach and for a treat. I jumped off the settee and started whooping and dancing on my hind legs, (that looks so cute I must say), and shouting 'Yes! Oh yes please! Please can I go, can I please?'

'Of course he can go out with you, Mum. Is Engle in the car?' asked Newmum.

'Oh yes,' said Nanny, and I started whooping and dancing again because Engle was my bestest friend in the whole wide world ever!

Newmum put my lead on me and then me and Nanny went out to the car. And there was Engle doing his own kind of whooping and dancing in the back of the car, while Grandad, sitting in the front, yelled at Engle to calm down, but he didn't. I climbed in the car and soon both me and Engle are whooping and jumping, smelling each other's bottoms and having a jolly splendid reunion.

'Are you sure about this?' Grandad asked Nanny as he turned on the car. The car started jumping and whooping too but I think this is because Grandad turned it on wrong, not because it was happy to be going to the beach for a treat!

'They're excited to see each other again, they'll soon settle down. Let's get a move on, I need that sea breeze on my face.' So, off we went and me and Engle stood up to look out of the back window at Newmum who was waving goodbye. I was a bit put out to see that she wasn't crying, in fact, she didn't look the least bit upset that I was going to the beach and to get a treat without her.

We hadn't been going too long when the car started whooping and jumping again, (I've no idea why as nobody had said anything nice to it), and Grandad's straw hat fell off. Then the car recovered itself and continued to go smoothly along the road and we could see lots of trees and things the other side of the window. After a while, the car got over excited again and then stopped, just like that, no warning or anything, and me and Engle slid off the back seat and Grandad's hat fell off again.

'Oh dear,' said Grandad, 'I think we've broken down.' Excuse me, Grandad, but we haven't done anything, it's the stupid car that's broken! Grandad got out of the car and stared at it for a while before he kicked the front wheel and got out his talking bone thing. 'I've 'phoned the garage and they're sending someone out to help us – won't take long. Soon be on the road again!'

Nanny sighed, and looked too hot and sweaty to even think about telling Grandad and the car off, and got out, taking me and Engle with her to sit on the grass beside the road. 'I was so looking forward to that ice cream treat as well.' Ice cream! So that was the treat part, lovely cool, drippy ice cream! I whined like hell 'cos it sounded like the treat thing was off. And all because the silly car had to attitudinize itself.

The car was sulking at the side of the road, nobody was of a mind to talk to it because it had spoilt a splendid afternoon, when I could suddenly hear the wonderful ding-dong music of an ice cream man's vehicle, and it was getting louder! And then we saw it come around the corner and Nanny jumped up to wave to the man and the man stopped and we were so very happy!

'You wanna the ice cream?' the man asked Nanny through his bushy moustache thing on top of his lip.

'Oh yes please! Four large whippy cornets thank you,' said Nanny, and I was pleased that she hadn't asked for a whippy cornet for the car who did not deserve one in the slightest.

Nanny and Grandad sat down again on the grass and, while they ate their whippy cornets, they each held one out for me and Engle. We loved the drippy ice cream and licked and licked as fast as we could but it still slid down their hands. Having scoffed the whippy cornets, we all laid down on the grass and dozed in the warm sun light. After a while, we heard another vehicle approaching, only this one sounded big and mean and the car started shaking with fright. Ha ha! Serves it right to be scared.

The big vehicle pulled the car and us all the way back to my house where Newmum met us at the door.

'What's happened?' asked Newmum, looking worried.

And before anyone else could answer, 'The car has been very naughty indeed and wore itself out showing off!' I barked and me and Engle ran into the house and down the hall.

Later that night, I was looking out of the window at the car and felt a bit sorry for it when Big Fat Black Cat weed all over its front wheel. That will stink for ages!

me whooping and dancing

Run Free Day

I was feeling rather cheesed off this morning, sort of miserable and mopey like for no reason I could put my paw on. It could have been the weather - it's rained for days and days and I haven't been out anywhere apart from the garden to do the usual. And even that's been a thoroughly unpleasant experience, trying to hold my beautiful bushy tail up in the air so that it doesn't get wet while doing my business. Doing a wee is just as bad. No sooner have I done it when the rain washes it all over my paws. The only bit of fun I've had all week is trying to dodge past Newmum to jump on the sofa before she's had time to clean my paws off with my bum towel!

Niko, the Big Fat Black Cat, has been no company either. When it rains he just sleeps and snores, very loudly. Big Fella had to turn the sound up on the colour box twice last night because of him.

I trudged into the kitchen for my breakfast, tail hanging very low so that Newmum could not help but notice that my cheese was definitely off. I don't know why humans use that expression for feeling fed up, as cheese is one of my most favourite snacks, except when Newmum sticks a worming tablet in it, hoping I won't notice.

By happy coincidence, Newmum was munching on cheese on toast and cut some up to go in my bowl along with the usual, boring boiled fish. I'm sick of boiled fish which I've been forced to eat, thanks to that interfering vet, since I had a patch of dry skin on my tummy. Why we continue to seek his opinion about my minor ailments is beyond me as his answer to everything is either a tablet stuck in a lump of cheese or boring boiled fish. And, now that I'm more grown up, I don't care to have my willy looked at anymore and he can stick his biscuits.

As I was tucking into my breakfast, Newmum opened the back door and sniffed the air.

'It's going to be a lovely day, Berts. The sun is shining and it's stopped raining at last. How about a walk on the beach?' Yippee! I scoffed the rest of my breakfast in double time - even the boring boiled fish – and started leaping around the kitchen and then dashed up and down the hall. (You must put on a good show just in case the humans think you've forgotten what the jangling of the lead means.)

In no time at all we're at the beach and I'm enjoying the feel of the sand beneath (and in between) my paws and Newmum takes off my lead.

'Off you go Berts! Run free!' And I did just that.

Birth Day

Today was a very special day. I woke up to cheese on toast, lots of hugs and kisses from Newmum, and a piece of card with writing on it that I wasn't allowed to chew. Big Fella gave me a parcel that I was allowed to chew and, joy of joys, it contained a new toy with lots of squeakers! It's called a Daisy and squeaks no matter where I sink my teeth. Big Fella chucked it up the hall and I dashed after it, grabbed it and then refused to let Big Fella take it back. After all, it was mine and if he liked it so much he should have one of his own.

After my cheese on toast breakfast, I took Daisy out into the garden and proceeded to rip apart her petals to get the annoying little squeakers out when I noticed something shiny and golden, flapping about near the barrel thing Newmum calls a pond. So, I dropped Daisy and had a good sniff to investigate. It wasn't very big but smelt rather good and, to stop it flapping about, I bit it quite hard! Yuck! It tasted disgusting and its scaly bits stuck to my teeth. I spat and coughed, chucked the stupid thing onto the grass, picked up Daisy and trotted back indoors.

Oh dear! The shiny golden scaly thing happened to be Newmum's favourite old goldfish who had the occasional habit of jumping out of the pond. His name was Hannibal, (because he had scoffed all his previous companions I later found out), and he had been very lucky in the past, when springing from the pond, as Newmum or the Big Fella were there to dump him back in the barrel before he gasped his last. I was, obviously, unaware of this and my canine gnashers had soon put an end to Hannibal's out of pond activities.

Newmum made such a fuss about the stupid fish and looked at me, very sternly like.

'If it wasn't for the fact that it's your birthday, I'd lock you up in your kennel cage', she sobbed as she dug a small hole in the grass and popped Hannibal into it. I think she'd intended to bury Hannibal but that turned out to be a complete waste of time as Niko (the Big Fat Black Cat) came along later, dug him up and scoffed him, right down to the last little bone. That cat will eat anything!

Birth Day! It was my birthday! That accounted for the Daisy thing and the cheese on toast for brekkers. And, that's not all, I was having a party! Newmum had laid the dining room table with lots of lovely scrummy things to eat like sausages and cheese, and some not so scrummy things like little waxy sticks that she later set fire to. The Big Fella looked exhausted and I think that may have had something to do with all the coloured rubber things Newmum had made him blow into. Still, I didn't care because the big coloured rubber things looked lovely, floating around the room. And then the doorbell rang and I barked like mad and all the little humans from next door came in and gave me more card things, (I wasn't allowed to chew these), and little parcels, (I was allowed to chew these). Inside the parcels were biscuits, a bone, and some foul-smelling stick things but I licked the little humans all the same.

Ding-dong! The doorbell rang again and this time it was Nana and Gramps and, my bestest friend in the whole wide world, their dog Engle. We barked and jumped at each other and sniffed each other's bums and ran into the garden. I showed Engle Hannibal's desecrated grave and we sniggered to think of the trouble Niko the BFBC would be in when Newmum discovered that he's scoffed what was left of the poor little dead fish.

Back inside, there were more card things not to chew and parcels to absolutely chew, and I got so excited that I weed on the carpet and was not told off because it was my birthday. Everyone had to wear little shiny hats, (including me and Engle and the elastic was very irritating), and then sing to me something about a Hippy day and then shout Hoorah! Nana then brought in a strange looking, sausage shaped cake thing with waxed sticks poked into it.

'Look Bertie,' she said, 'I've made this cake to look like you!' The poor woman is obviously getting old and suffering from catajacks because the cake is plainly two Swiss rolls stuck together and covered in brown stuff. She then set fire to the waxed sticks and Newmum blew them out and didn't even get told off.

'Make a wish, Berts' said Newmum. And I did, but I'm not telling because otherwise it won't come to be true.

Then me and Engle got to sit at the table with all the little humans from next door and we munched all the sausages and cake. It was brilliant and I hope it's my birthday again tomorrow.

me
(happy)

Pond thing

Help!
Help!

Hannibal

Squeak

Squeak

Daisy

Snow Day

I woke up this morning and couldn't believe my eyes! What was Newmum thinking of? For some reason, she had covered the garden in that white stuffing that comes out of my toys when I rip out the sqeakers. Eeeek! Did that mean she had ripped up all my toys without my permission? I dashed to the toy box to check only to find everything accounted for, even the old socks. So where did Newmum get all the white stuff from? This called for further investigation.

I ran to the back door and bashed at the cat flap. This had become an accepted command in our household, (humans are very easy to train you know), I bash the cat flap and Newmum or Big Fella opens the door and I run out. And, when I want to come back in, I poke the cat flap from the outside and they rush to open the door again to allow my re-entry. They must be quick, an immediate response in fact, otherwise I stand at the door and howl pitifully and then the neighbours come out and say 'Poor little Bertie's been left out in the cold', or something very similar. I'm sure they would phone the RSPCA if necessary.

Anyway, Newmum opened the door and I looked out into the garden and, bloody hell, there was loads of the white stuff everywhere. It was in the flower pots, all over the grass and even on the shed roof. Newmum must have got up very early to do all this, I thought, and for what? It couldn't be that she didn't have enough to do, after all, she was always going on at Big Fella about how the day didn't have the right number of hours in it and that he was lazy. I did not agree with this however, the Big Fat Black Cat is lazy, but Big Fella is always on the go. Sometimes he gets up from the sofa three or four times in the evening to fiddle with the colour box.

I leapt out over the doorstep into the white stuff and ran down the garden, barking my head off and wagging my tail like mad. And then I discovered that I was wet. Very wet and very, very cold. This was not right at all and I was not happy. The white stuff was turning to water as I stepped on it and was quite slippery, so much so that I slid the rest of the way down the garden on my bum! I quickly checked to make sure no one had seen this, as it was an embarrassing moment for me, and I am usually so elegant and agile, as well as being adorable in every way. It was time to make an orderly retreat into the house and to my plump cushion in front of the living room fire.

From his elevated position on the sofa, the BFBC purred and sniggered as he stuck one leg in the air and licked his nether regions.

'What's so funny, Fish Face?' I whined as I turned over on my cushion to dry my chest in front of the fire.

'I shall never forget your face, scraggy puppy, as you went sliding down the garden on your bum through the snow. Quite made my morning, that did!'

'Snow! What's snow?' I sat up abruptly and cocked my ears, ready for another load of verbal rubbish from Niko. Why do cats lie so much? It doesn't do them any favours.

'The white stuff, stupid puppy! It's called snow and when you see it in the garden you do not go out for any reason. No one goes out. The fire will stay on all day long and we must snooze, while making appropriate snoozy noises of course. Then we get stroked and fed more than usual, although I'm not altogether sure why humans do this.'

Blow me! For once, Big Fat Black Cat was telling the truth and we spent a lovely day, snoozing and eating, and we didn't go outside once. I don't know where Niko went to do a wee, but I did mine behind the sofa where it's very dark and, more importantly, very private. Besides, it won't start to smell for ages yet.

Facebook Day

Ha ha! I've done it! I now have my very own Facebook page and am a very lucky boy because I have seventeen friends. Mind you, I've never met most of them in my life before but that doesn't matter because they all write very nice things about me.

I have been watching my mum for months tip tapping away on her lapdog pewter and, when she went off to have a bath this morning (and left the lapdog pewter on), I decided to have a go myself. I soon discovered that my cute little paws were too big to tap at the different buttons as I kept pressing loads of the flipping things at the same time! And then I had a brainwave – I needed a pointy thing!

A pointy thing is what my mum uses to write in little boxes in her mewspaper. Sometimes you have to bite the end and chew it a bit. I don't think Mum likes the taste very much as after she's chewed it she usually scribbles with the pointy thing all over the little boxes, screws up the mewspaper, throws it in the bin and puts the kettle on.

I found a pointy thing, covered in dust (and my fur would you believe), under a kitchen cupboard together with an old dog biscuit that had gone soft (and tasted quite nice now actually), and held it in my mouth while I leapt back up to the LDP. (I'm not writing 'lapdog pewter' anymore because it takes too long and I might get bored). It worked brilliantly and I could tap the buttons one at a time. There's one tiny drawback – holding the pointy thing makes me drool and I have to keep stopping to lick the buttons clean.

And that was that! I was away – entering all my finer details onto my FB page (that's Facebook page and I'm not writing that all the time either!). Here are some of my entries:

Name:
Bertie Boy Baroni

Date of birth:
I had to tell a fib here as FB has no understanding of dog years!

Likes:
Chasing next door's cat, eating, sleeping, going for walks, ripping the annoying squeakers out of my soft toys, cheese and bones

Hobbies:
Chasing next door's cat, eating, sleeping, going for walks, and ripping the annoying squeakers out of my soft toys

Favourite TV/Film:
Wallace and Grommit

The Incredible Journey (but not the cat), Harry Potter (because Mum always watches this in bed)

Favourite music:
The Ice Cream Van

Favourite books:
My diary

Favourite quote:
A bobo is not just for Christmas
Bertie Boy Baroni December 2008)

Status:
Single

Profile statement:
I'm just about the cutest boy you will ever encounter and am clever, happy and content. I find cats to

be sly and terrible liars and I
hate the rain.

Job done! Now I can't wait until tomorrow to go back onto FB – it's not cool, apparently, to stay on there too long at any one time as your FB friends might think you are very sad.

Facebook Day 2

I am in the proverbial 'dog house'! Mum has discovered my FB activity and is threatening Parental Controls (whoever they are) and I'm sure I won't like them! And how is it my fault that lots of fat ladies wearing no clothes, and sitting on dining room chairs backwards, want to be my friends?

Facebook Day 3

There's just no pleasing some people! Now Newmum is very unhappy about the very attractive thin ladies who want to be my friends. They are wearing bikinis and are lying in rivers or in the big puddle! What's wrong with that for dog's sake! Personally, I don't like getting wet.

Facebook Day 4

We have reached a compromise. Newmum has a turn on FB and then I have a turn. Newmum is not happy (again) because I have more friends than her, in fact she is outraged that some of my friends did not ask her to be their friend. I cannot see the problem as she is beginning to look and act a bit stretched and wrinkled (only round the eyes it must be said) while I am just so cute and adorable! Who would you want to be friends with? Lol...... that means 'laugh out loud' which I can't do, obviously. This'll make you lol, Newmum thought it meant 'lots of love'! How sad is that! Actually, it's quite nice really, come to think of it.

Facebook Day 5

Friend Jonathan has asked to borrow my profile picture to try and 'entice some ladies'. I said he could and now there are two very cute little boys on FB!

I had a message from friend Jonathan to say it didn't work and he is still 'lady-less' and has gone back to his original chubby boy image. I think he would do well as a stand-up funny person, they don't care what they look like.

Facebook Day 6

What a shock! I had a fit today, just couldn't control my legs, face, tongue, nothing! I was shaking like a leaf and tried to cling to Newmum for all I was worth! Newmum and Big Fella both tried to grab the telling bone to speak to that vet person and Newmum won! Then I was rushed to the car and we sped off to the vet's house through the most horrible thunder and lightning you could possibly imagine! Newmum said this was just like Frankenstein and that she'd created a monster. I had no idea what she was talking about.

When we arrived, I felt fine, the fit had passed, and I was back to my adorable and cute self. The vet was not convinced and insisted on giving me a full, and I mean 'full', examination. Come on, the willy bit is great but the thermometer up your bum is going a little too far! Then he made me run around the car park in the rain! Has he not read my FB profile!

So, there I was, soaking wet and going curly, 'infiltrated' and feeling quite miffed, with Newmum crying and the Big Fella looking white as a sheet, while the vet was looking very pleased with himself.

'He appears to be over the fit and is, on the whole, a very healthy young dog. No heart or breathing problems and his mobility is excellent! If I didn't know better, I'd say he'd been on his computer for too long! Ha ha ha!' The vet laughed like a drain (what a strange expression)! Our drain never laughs, it just stinks. Newmum and I looked at each other in a very 'knowing' way and then Newmum grabbed me and squeezed me so very tight.

'Just keep a diary of any unusual activity,' (Newmum and I exchanged further 'knowing' looks), 'just in case we have to medicate later on. But, on the whole, I think this chap is fine. Here you go boy,' and the vet gave me some revolting brown crunchy bits. I ate them just to be sociable, it was an emergency appointment after all.

Big Fella paid the vet with his plastic and looked very upset! 'Why can't he be ill during normal vet hours for God's sake? That's just cost me a fortune!'

'But he's worth it! Poor little boy, you must be so hungry' and Newmum cuddled me real tight.

'Me too! How about we pick up some fried chicken and chips on the way home?'

'Good idea! I'm sure Berts will like it!'

Me and Big Fella loved the fried chicken and chips. However, Newmum was up all night regurgitating said chicken and chips. Me and Big Fella took some great pictures! FB here we come!

Squirty Bum Day

I couldn't believe what was happening to me today and felt very sick. This is terribly difficult for me to put into words as I am so upset and embarrassed, but here goes.

I have lost control of my poo! It just squirts out of my bum whenever it feels like it and Newmum gets upset and tells me I am a poor boy and then proceeds to hold up my tail and wipe my bum with some oily cloth things she calls babbly wipes. And, if that wasn't enough for a poor chap to contend with, she then washes my bum and makes my tail and legs all wet. What's going on?

Then my nanna arrived, (that's Newmum's mum and Engle's mum and I'm fed up with trying to remember a whole family tree every five minutes so have decided to call her nanna for short), and my mortifying indiscretions of the morning were relayed to her. She immediately sorted the situation.

I am feeling much better now and have discovered that my recent bout of funny tum and squirty bum was down to the stupidity of Newmum. You see, to keep my coat and skin in such fine condition, I was recently prescribed very special oily capsizeables from my vet (you remember him, nice chap who feels you all over, looks at your willy and then gives you a biscuit). They are very expensive and I know this because Newmum pays for them with her plastic card while looking very sad but I am worth it. So, when we ran out, Newmum went and bought some cheap fish oil squashy things from a large shop that is German (I know this because I am a dachshund). Newmum gave me some last week and they were horrid and made my chicken smell like fish when she squirted the oil over my dinner. Nanna says that Newmum should only have given me one every two weeks and not one EVERY DAY!!!!!

Since Newmum has had to clear up my mess and wash my bottom each time I had an accident I think she has been suitably punished for being such a nit wit. She has also been feeding some to the Big Fella, (his have garlic in), and I think Newmum has made another mistake here because, if he gets a funny tum, she is in for a very bad time indeed as he is huge and they don't do babbly wipes in his size, I'm sure! Ha ha ha!

However, I am now having a lovely day and am being cuddled quite a lot and will soon have some sausages for my dinner, but not the horrible vegetable things and no smelly fish oil!

The Kissmas Time - part one

the turkeybird

BANG!

kissmas bang thing

Kissmas hat

This is a very odd time of year, ending with what Humans call 'Kissmas Day' which involves no kissing or licking whatsoever!

It all starts when the heating goes off about a week before the big day and Newmum shouts down the talking bone and a little man turns up an hour later with a smelly bag of metal things. I recognise him as the same little man who popped round a couple of days before and said that everything was 'Tickerty boo'. He shuts himself in the bathroom, (probably because Newmum is a bit scary when she is in her shouting mood), and makes a lot of noise. Newmum then makes him a cup of tea to make up for the shouting but he doesn't come out of the bathroom. I don't blame him because when Newmum shouts at me I won't look at her for a couple of hours at least and anyway, tea tastes disgusting.

After a while there is loud banging and clanking coming from the bathroom followed by a small explosion and the little man comes out with a very dirty face, while shaking quite a bit which makes it difficult for him to drink his disgusting tea. After a few sips he tells Newmum (who, by this time, is looking very scary indeed) that he must go off to buy an incontrovertible female diaphragm stipulatoriser and will be straight back to fix the boiler. I think he is making this up just to escape and Newmum doesn't look entirely convinced either but reluctantly lets him leave the house, on the condition that she keeps his smelly bag of metal things until he returns. That woman trusts no one!

The little man comes back later that afternoon with his incontrovertible female diaphragm stipulatoriser in a brown paper bag (looking very happy with himself) and tries to pat my head. I just growl at him as I'm the one who's had to put up with Newmum's shouty scary mood, and I've had no elevenses or lunch because she was too busy stomping and banging around the house complaining about being cold. Anyway, in no time at all the little man fixes the boiler with the thingy in the brown paper bag and Newmum and I are soon so hot that I'm lying with my head sticking out the cat flap and she's wandering around in a vest and shorts!

A couple of days later Newmum goes out for ages and returns with loads and loads of bags. It takes her about half an hour to carry all the bags in from the car and then she starts shouting down the talking bone again, this time I think it's at Big Fella because she's going on about doing everything around here and all he ever seems to do is pick up my number twos from the garden. This is not entirely correct as he does do the hoovering occasionally, like yesterday, and breaks the Hoover, like in the summer, and will probably buy Newmum a fresh one, like on her birthday, and she will go bonkers. Oh well.

Once Newmum has emptied all the things from the bags and stuffed most of them in cupboards around the kitchen, she tries to hide some of the things by wrapping them up in very colourful paper and placing them around the indoor-outdoor tree. In lots of ways, Newmum is quite intelligent, for a human that is, but this seems to me a stupid idea as Big Fella is bound to notice all those bright packages as soon as he walks in, unless he develops catajacks before he comes home.

I'm having a good sniff at the packages and the indoor-outdoor tree when Newmum shouts at me from the kitchen 'Leave those things alone, Bertie!' (What with her supersonic hearing and the fact that she can see through solid walls, it never ceases to amaze me why that woman isn't out catching criminals and saving the world! But there again, I suppose me and Big Fella need her more).

The indoor-outdoor tree is a fascinating thing, for most of the year it sits outside on the patio and then for the Kissmas Time it comes in and sits in the living room beside the television. Newmum makes it feel really welcome by hanging lots of pretty things on it and then covers it with twinkly lights and gives it a drink. Big Fat Black Cat does his business in its pot when the humans are in bed. I thought he was being naughty, but he told me to the tree it was a welcoming feast and that he'd been doing this for the past seven years so he must be right. I just think that it's lovely for everyone to take so much trouble to make sure that the indoor-outdoor tree isn't lonely during the Kissmas Time.

Over the next couple of days even Big Fella tries to hide things wrapped up in coloured paper around the indoor-outdoor tree and Newmum pretends not to notice, she can be quite understanding at times. Some of the packages smell absolutely delicious and I find myself drooling every time I pass the tree on route to my toy box. What are they trying to hide under there for dog's sake!

The Kissmas Day Eve arrives along with Newmum's pup who is called

Prodigal. (That's what Big Fella calls him and it has something to do with a story in The Book about coming home and fat calves everywhere.). He is very tall and very funny. I like him a lot because he sees no need to get out of bed until absolutely necessary, and sometimes not even then, (although I'm pretty sure Newmum didn't empty all the paper out of the bin thing for that!). He makes Newmum cry and laugh all at the same time and makes Big Fella sigh a lot. And me, he loves me and calls me 'Babe Magnet' and takes me for a long walk around town and down by the sea where we run into lots of female humans, whose names we don't know, but who are very nice and one even bought Prodigal and me food and drinks. He's my almost bestest pal, although Engle is my bestest pal ever, and I do love sausages!

Later that evening Newmum made Prodigal put on his hat and coat to accompany her to the Midnight thingy as Big Fella wouldn't go even though, she said, he'd been tizered as a Catholic. Big Fella said it was nothing to do with him as his dad had sneaked him off to a Catholic church without his mum knowing so it didn't count. I was half asleep and very warm and didn't take too much notice. Big Fat Black Cat was in the kitchen gnawing at the frozen turkey bird. What a silly billy! It's much better cooked!

During the Kissmas night, me and Big Fat Black Cat shared a chocolate bobble thingy that was hanging from the indoor-outdoor tree. BFBC then had to go outside for squirty relief, (he's really not used to the rich things of life), while I finished off the cheese and biscuits Prodigal had left next to the settee, but not the pickled onions.

Kissmas morning and what joy! Everyone, including Prodigal, got up and sat around the indoor-outdoor tree and pretended they hadn't noticed all the bright, colourful packages that had been sitting there for days. (The whole lot of them are developing catajacks as far as I'm concerned!) Newmum gave us all, including the BFBC, a package to tear apart to discover what was inside and, joy of joys, mine was a lovely new, squeaking, long, pink, hairy thing which was just what I'd always wanted for the longest time ever in my life! (Mind you, I've no idea what it is.) Big Fella unwrapped his to find some circle things he likes to watch on the emceedeeveedee player when everyone has gone to bed. Prodigal was over the moon with his new personal talking bone machine effort thing that took pictures from people. Big Fat Black Cat was positively kittenish about his grey, lifelike, catnip mouse. Newmum, however, looked a bit sad when she unwrapped her flashing, novelty reindeer earrings. (I thought they went really well with her novelty red, cooking person's hat but you just can't please some people!)

The big hot cooking cupboard in the kitchen is doing its stuff! No one had noticed that the BFBC had been gnawing at the turkey bird and Newmum plonked it in the hot cupboard having covered it in bacon and other stuff. The smell is just to die for! Big Fella presented Newmum with a nice package (that wasn't under the indoor-outdoor tree) containing a collar that made her cry as she tried to do it up around her wrist, not because it didn't fit but because it was just so beautiful and sparkly! Big Fella looked very pleased with himself and gave Prodigal a 'look'. Next thing, Prods has pulled a small, red wrapped parcel from his jeans' pocket and, lo and behold, Newmum is crying again as she is trying to poke some extra_sparkly things into her ears. Come on people – what's wrong with a packet of five flavoured chew sticks for dog's sake! They are very tasty and don't make you cry.
To be continued...

The 'indoor-outdoor' tree

The Kissmas Time

BFBC pooh!! yuk!

Shiny boxes (smells good)

Present from Big Fella x J

The Kissmas Time - part two

More presents

Bong! Bong!

noisy clock thing

I am now sick and tired of eating the cooked turkey bird. There is no end to the wretched stuff and my heart sinks each time Newmum opens the very cold cupboard and I see it sitting there, looking just as big as it ever was. Even Prodigal, who could eat for England, has turned his nose up at the latest round of turkey bird sandwiches. Big Fella suggested that we have ham sandwiches instead and Newmum found a ham tin in one of her cupboards. However, on closer inspection, Prodigal declared that it was not suitable for human consumption because it said 'nineteen ninety-six' on the lid, but Newmum opened it anyway. It smelt disgusting, even worse than the expired rat I'd found under the shed last week. (The rat had been dead for ages but I pretended it wasn't and shook it violently anyway. You must shake rats violently to stop them biting you with their nasty little front teeth). So, that was that for the ham tin, it wasn't suitable for dog consumption either (thank goodness), and the smell of it had made Big Fat Black Cat dive out through the cat flap! I took that to be a no no from him as well.

Nobody does very much during the rest of the Kissmas Time, which is okay for me as I don't do an awful lot at any other time, but it can irritate a chap somewhat when he goes to jump in his favourite chair for the mid-afternoon snooze only to find said chair occupied by Big Fella having his mid-afternoon snooze. He has a huge comfy bed all his very own so why he can't do the snooze thing in that I don't know! Prods is busy with his new talking bone up in his bedroom. He taps out messages on it and then holds it in his hand, watching it intently, until it makes a funny noise and lights up which means the thing has thought up an answer. It must be telling him some very interesting things as he doesn't even want me to play 'Babe Magnet' down the sea front.

Zipperdeedoodah! Even before the sound of the doorbell, I could hear my bestest pal in the whole wide world scratching and barking outside and me and Newmum rushed to open the front door. Hoorah! There was Nanny and Grandad and Engle! What a relief to turkey bird sandwiches and doing nothing! Me and Engle ran down the hall to the living room, barking and jumping all over Big Fella, (Engle likes him loads), and then Engle ran into the kitchen and weed up the very cold cupboard even before I'd had a chance to tell him about the never-ending turkey bird! He's so clever!

Newmum wasn't very happy about the wee but Nanny just laughed and said that Engle was excited at coming to visit so it wasn't his fault really. (Mind you, I get excited about visiting Nanny and I've never weed up her very cold cupboard but I didn't say anything). Big Fella, Prodigal and Grandad were shaking each other's hands and patting each other on the back, although no one had been coughing so they were probably doing that just in case. And then Nanny pulled out loads more brightly coloured packages from her big bag (that looks like a carpet folded in half) and gave one to all of us while Newmum found some for Nanny, Grandad and Engle from under the indoor-outdoor tree. Once everyone had ripped off the lovely paper, me and Engle took all the coloured paper into the hall and tore it to shreds and tossed it high into the air and jumped and rolled in it. Such fun! And when we took a breather, I looked at the hall carpet, or where the hall carpet should have been, and there was this lovely sea of Kissmas brightness and joyful stuff! The Kissmas Time is great when Engle is here.

Teatime was splendid! Nanny had brought some real ham and Newmum made sausage rolls and got the cheese out of the very cold cupboard. I love cheese almost more than sausages. Everyone ate lots and lots and then Grandad fell asleep in my favourite chair but we had to wake him up again because Nanny said it was time for the Kissmas quiz. Prods groaned and said he was going to his bedroom but Newmum said he wasn't, (in that tone of voice she uses that makes Big Fella go a bit pale).

During the quiz, Grandad made everyone laugh with his funny answers, Big Fella sulked about his wrong answers, Prods amazed everyone with his right answers, and Nanny and Newmum argued over a 'technicality'. They are so competitive!

Next came Newmum's favourite game of 'charades' (whatever they are) but she is very enthusiastic about this game and, apparently, is very good at it because she used to work on a stage jumping around and wearing funny clothes. Prods also likes this game because he is an actor. (He has been in something called 'Doctor Who' three times but Newmum says you never see his face so does it really count?) Nanny likes this game because she thinks she's good at it while Big Fella and Grandad are absolutely useless. However, very soon everyone is laughing and that's all that matters for the Kissmas Time.

The visitors are staying the night and everyone drinks lots of the funny juice (except me and Engle) and get louder and louder as the night goes on. Our next-door neighbours come in and join everyone in drinking the funny juice and don't notice that their beagle pup Bailey is covering me and Engle with his slobber! Don't get me wrong, Bailey is a lovely pup but is three times the size of me and Engle and talks about fox hunting all the time and his breath stinks! Me and Engle tried to tell him that fox hunting was banned like a hundred years ago, but he didn't take any notice. Some things are so inbred.

What's the matter with everyone? No one seems to want to go to bed and it's getting very late! Me and Engle are so tired that we decide to have a snooze behind the settee. Grandad is, once again, asleep in my favourite chair; Prods' new talking bone is flashing on and off like no dog's business and he can't keep up with the tip tapping messages; Newmum and Nanny are singing songs with the neighbours and

Bailey has been sent home in disgrace. Newmum was saving those chocolates for the next time she feels ill! Then Big Fella shouts out that the countdown has started and everyone goes quiet while we listen to the television going 'Bong! Bong! Bong!'

Happy New Year! We are all so excited and kissing people from up and down the road. Well, I'm not but Big Fella, Nanny and Grandad and Prods are, along with the neighbours. Me and Engle are running up and down barking like mad while Newmum is ringing a large bell for all she's worth, bless her! Firework things are exploding into the air and making lovely patterns on the night sky and everyone is so very happy! Everyone, that is, except Bailey who is being sick because he ate Newmum's 'Next time I'm ill' chocolates. Still, I expect he enjoyed them at the time.

We've just finished breakfast, a splendid feast of bacon, sausages, black pudding (which I like almost more than cheese), eggs (which you can keep), tomatoes and beans (we won't even go there)! Prods is now carrying Nanny's carpet bag out to the car while she squeezes his face and gives him some paper stuff to put in his pocket for a 'rainy day'. Prods is very happy and looks around to make sure Newmum hasn't noticed while Big Fella and Grandad shake hands and pat each other's backs again, (there are still no signs of bad coughs so the patting must be working). Newmum and Nanny hug for the longest time ever and me and Engle do the 'Bum Sniff'. The car disappears into the distance, Prods sets off for the station with his talking bone still in his hand, (and what Big Fella calls a bag of booty on his back), while we return into the house.

I don't mind telling you that the end of the Kissmas Time is quite welcome really. Big Fat Black Cat comes back in from the shed, Big Fella goes back to work every day, Newmum stops crying and that flipping indoor-outdoor tree goes back outside where it belongs! Those prickly needle things were killing me!

My Finale

Not been too well lately. My back is playing me up again and I can't leap and jump in excitement when Big Fella shakes my lead and says 'Come on Berts! Walkies!' Of course, I go on the walks to keep him company because he'll be lonely otherwise. Even though I don't feel well I'm still very thoughtful.

I've been to the vet's a lot recently as well and Newmum is always watching me and stroking my lovely little head. (Dachshunds have beautiful and well defined heads that are a pleasure to stroke – unlike cats who have short stubby heads and when you go to stroke them they say 'Don't touch me'.) Even the vet's visits are not the same. He doesn't look at my willy anymore – just not interested – and instead of a treat I get stuff squirted down my throat through a plastic tube. Newmum keeps giving me dollops of pate and lumps of cheese thinking I don't know that there is a nasty tasting object tablet thing hidden in the middle. I can't understand why she's so surprised when I suck off the pate and cheese and spit out the nasty tasting object tablet thing! Who wouldn't!

And things aren't the same since Big Fat Black Cat disappeared. There one minute – gone the next! Newmum's young'un Prods came to stay and there was a lot of crying and then me and BFBC were given sausages with a lighted candle thing poked in them – which was very silly because we couldn't get near the sausages. Then Prods blew out the candle things and we could eat the sausages while Newmum and Prods started singing something about a bird day. (I do wonder about those two sometimes.) BFBC had been shrinking and was half his usual size so I suppose he wasn't Big Fat Black Cat anymore.

And then he said 'Tuck in Baby Puppy – it's my Kitten Day'. I think his eyesight was shrinking as well because I wasn't a puppy anymore being eleventy-one and he certainly wasn't a kitten!

The next morning Newmum and Prods put the not so BFBC into the pet carrier and went out with it. They came back about an hour later looking all blotchy and their eyes were swollen and they had an empty pet carrier! I just assumed they had been fighting and the not so BFBC had scarpered. I don't like shouting or fighting so I don't blame him. But I do miss him.

I'm feeling very sick today and can't make my legs move properly but I can still drag myself into the garden to do my business – unlike the last days of the BFBC who did his behind the sofa! But all is not good – I have a squirty bum and Newmum's calling Big Fella who's still in bed.

I'm now wrapped in a blanket and Newmum is cuddling me so tight I can't breathe – Big Fella is talking to the phone thing and then I remember it's Saturday and I should be having toast and jam with Newmum in bed before I jump all over the paper she's looking at.

Big Fella says to Newmum that we can go now or wait until after ten which will be cheaper. Newmum screams 'He can't wait until ten! We must go now!'.

I'm in the car on Newmum's lap still wrapped in my blanket and she's crying so much that I wonder what Prods has done now to upset her so much. (He upsets her a lot – even when you can't see him.) Big Fella is steering the car very fast because there are no other cars about – I think most people are in bed eating toast and jam instead of steering cars.

Oh, for Dog's sake! We're at the vet's and I try to bark my disapproval but only a little whimper escapes my throat – what is wrong with me! Newmum carries me into the vet's which is all in darkness apart from the poking room we go into. The vet is a lovely young human female and I think to myself that Prods would like her very much and could have young'uns with her quite easily. She lays me on her vet platform and gives me a very, and I mean very, thorough examination. I can't move so I must endure the pokes and prods and the glass thing stuck up my bum and then everyone has to be very quiet while she listens to my heart.

I'm getting very tired and my body hurts so I close my eyes but I hear the vet lady say that it would be the kindest thing to do. I'm not sure what she's on about but it makes Newmum cry even harder and she squeezes me so tight. I open my eyes and – blow me! – Big Fella is crying so much that snot stuff is coming out of his big nose which is enough to put anyone off their toast and jam.

The vet lady puts a needle in the scruff of my neck and then I begin to feel better and I think I want to go to sleep now. It's so cosy here with Newmum cuddling me and Big Fella stroking my head – and I don't feel shaky anymore. This is a nice feeling.

My dad is calling me and I look up to the ceiling and there he is – just like when he used to visit me at the puppy run.

"Are you ready Berts – ready to run with me?" and he wags his beautiful tail and paws the air.

"Yes Dad – I'm ready. But can I come back after our run?"

"No son. We're going away together forever."

"Oh – okay Dad."

"Tell me Berts – have you had a good life?"

"The best Dad – the very best!"

I suddenly get up and move towards my dad – rising higher and higher – and then I can see Newmum and Big Fella below me still stroking the lovely, handsome little dachshund that was me – and still crying! (Where does all this human water come from?)

"Will they be okay Dad?" I ask as we slip out of the vet's poking room.

"Of course, they will, son. They have happy memories of their life with you – and, besides, they're going to adopt two black cats next week." In my surprise, I do a double somersault in the air at this extraordinary news and yelp somewhat loudly.

And then me and my dad are outside and we're running and leaping and laughing, rising higher and higher until we're amongst the clouds.

Bertie

2003 - 2014

Bertie's Words of Wisdom

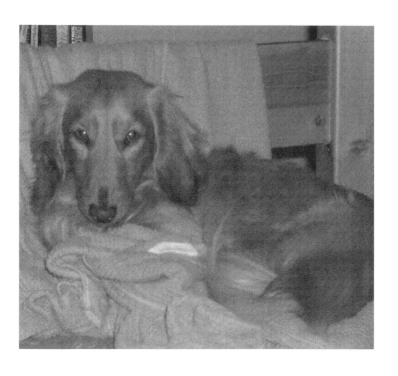

Me resting

Resting time is very important and you must do this at least seven times a day otherwise you will not be able to maintain your adorability.

Me on the beach

Walking along the beach is fun and the sand feels soft on the paws but it can make you drool a lot which is unattractive.

Me on the lapdog

Lapdogs and FB can be fun but don't stare at the screen for too long because it makes your eyes go squiffy which does nothing for your adorability.

Me resting again

When finding somewhere to rest make sure you get the lighting right so that it shows off your subtle fur tones because this is definitely attractive.

Me laughing

Always laugh at your humans' jokes otherwise they will feel silly and embarrassed and won't take you for a walk because they are sulking which is unattractive.

My favourite dinner

Sausages are my favourite dinner but
not the green and yellow and orange
bits which taste disgusting and have an
adverse effect on one's adorability.

My pal Engle

Engle is my bestest pal in the whole wide world ever and is scruffy and scampy which can be quite attractive but not in the same way that I am attractive.

Me looking handsome

When being photographed always try to look as handsome as possible unlike Newmum's passport picture which made her cry and is scary and very unattractive.

About the Author

Davina Baron lives and works in East Anglia and her writing style is both poignant and humorous - she can hit you where it hurts with her emotionally packed short stories.

Bertie's Diary is Davina's first published book, charting the day to day thoughts of her beloved miniature dachshund who shared her life for many years.

To keep up to date on Davina's writing and follow her on social media please go to https://www.facebook.com/Davina-Baron-Author-356351074764371/

Dear Reader

If you have enjoyed reading about Bertie, then please tell your friends and relatives and leave a review on Amazon. Thank you.

Printed in Great Britain
by Amazon